How to Easily Prepare and Eat Healthier *for Medical Professionals*

Learn how to keep yourself and your family healthy by buying, preparing, and serving nutritious meals and snacks.

Table of Contents

Dedication

This book is dedicated to Farell Moughon, my husband, who supports me in all my endeavors and Reba Taylor Muhlnickel, my best sister/friend who didn't get to see the finished product.

Testimonials

"I recommend Jane's health class. I learned something every week. Her lessons give you lots of information. She's well prepared and excellent teacher." Linda Garcia

"Her class empowers me to take control of my health through informed choices, and her class equips us with real world nutrition knowledge that can be easily applied to our daily lives leading to a healthier and happier life." Bonnie Mathieu.

"This class has been life changing for me with positive long lasting changes to my health and well being. Her expertise in this field and valuable insights are brought to the subject matter. I am much more vigilant now about food ingredients and what I eat." Mary Lou Williams

"I am amazed at all the information that she included in these classes. She is experienced and inspiring." Ann Goodwin

"The class is new beginnings toward better health and well being. Jane is a very knowledgeable teacher and presents the class in a very informative way. I have learned so much about food and am eating healthier." Dorris Harris

"Jane's healthy eating class is very comprehensive with valuable information. Her knowledge and ability to consolidate the many sources provides an excellent source to help individuals avoid the many ingredients that do damage to our bodies." Cathy Sterling

Introduction

Why I Wrote This Book

As a health and nutrition coach with over 35 years of experience, I've seen firsthand how powerful proper nutrition is in preventing and even reversing chronic health conditions. Yet, when I started looking into how much nutritional education medical professionals receive, I was stunned. The average U.S. medical school includes only **19.6 hours of nutrition education** over four years of training. Nurses receive even less. Despite being on the front lines of patient care, **medical professionals** are rarely taught how to use food as medicine—yet they are expected to counsel patients on health and wellness.

I wrote ***A Medical Professionals' Guide to Easy Healthy Eating*** because I care deeply about those who dedicate their lives to healing others. As a nurse, physician assistant, medical technician, or any other healthcare provider, your time is precious. You work long shifts, often on rotating schedules, with little time to prepare nutritious meals. Too often, you are forced to rely on hospital cafeteria food, vending machines, or fast food— options that are often processed, high in unhealthy fats, and lacking in essential nutrients.

But here's the truth: **You can't pour from an empty cup.** You spend your days and nights caring for others, but your own health is just as important.

If you're run down, stressed, and fueling your body with nutrient-poor foods, it takes a toll—not just on your energy levels but on your long-term well-being. Many healthcare professionals struggle with burnout, weight gain, high blood pressure, and even metabolic issues—not because they don't care about health, but because they don't have the time or resources to focus on their own.

This book is here to change that. Inside, you'll find simple, realistic, and time-efficient ways to nourish yourself—even on the busiest days. You don't need hours in the kitchen, expensive organic groceries, or elaborate meal plans. You just need **easy, healthy strategies** that fit your life.

I want you to know that your health **matters.** You are a vital part of our healthcare system, and the world needs you—thriving, energetic, and well. My hope is that this book empowers you to prioritize yourself so that you can continue doing what you do best: helping others heal.

Let's get started on a path to **healthier, smarter eating—one simple step at a time. Ideas for feeding your family healthy meals and snacks have also been included in this book.**

As a medical professional, you want the best for you and your family—keeping them happy, healthy, and thriving. But with today's busy schedules, making nutritious meals can feel overwhelming. That's why I wrote *A Medical Professionals' Guide to Easy Healthy Eating*—to simplify grocery shopping and meal prep while helping you make healthier choices for you and your family. Our food supply is filled with unhealthy—and even dangerous—ingredients. Many products contain hidden sugars, artificial sweeteners, genetically modified ingredients, and harmful fats. Processed foods are stripped of essential nutrients, leading to deficiencies that can weaken the immune system, contribute to weight gain, and increase the risk of chronic diseases. By learning to read labels and choose whole, nourishing foods, you can take control of your and your family's health. You have the power to make informed choices that will fuel your and your family's well-being for years to come.

01

Chapter 1: Introduction to Budget-Friendly Healthy Eating

The Importance of Healthy Eating for Medical Professionals

Healthy eating is a cornerstone for medical professionals looking to thrive in today's fastpaced world. As a busy professional, you often juggle multiple responsibilities, from work to maybe your children's school activities, making it easy to overlook the importance of nutrition. However, prioritizing healthy eating can lead to improved energy levels, better focus for yourself and children, and a stronger immune system for the whole family. By making small, intentional changes to your diet, you can create a foundation for lifelong healthy habits that will benefit everyone.

One of the most significant advantages of healthy eating is its impact on overall well-being. Nutritious foods provide essential vitamins and minerals that support growth and development in children, while also helping adults maintain their health. Incorporating a variety of fruits, vegetables, whole grains, and lean proteins into your meals can enhance mood and promote better sleep patterns. When you nourish your body with wholesome foods, you pave the way for happier, more energetic days filled with shared laughter and activity.

Budget-friendly healthy eating is not just achievable; it can also be enjoyable. Planning meals together as a family can turn grocery shopping into a fun activity, where everyone's preferences are heard and catered to. Engaging your children, if any, in the kitchen not only teaches them valuable cooking skills but also encourages them to try new foods. By making healthy meals a family affair, you'll foster a positive relationship with food and instill a sense of pride in your dietary choices.

Moreover, healthy eating can significantly reduce long-term healthcare costs. When health professionals and families prioritize nutritious meals, they can help prevent chronic diseases, such as obesity, diabetes, and heart disease. While the initial investment in fresh, whole foods might seem daunting, the savings on medical bills and the overall improvement in quality of life can be substantial. By focusing on budget-friendly, healthy eating now, you are setting yourself and your family up for a brighter, healthier future.

Ultimately, the importance of healthy eating for yourself and your families cannot be overstated. It is a powerful tool that fosters physical health, emotional stability, and family bonding. As you navigate the challenges of busy life, remember that making conscious, healthy choices can lead to a wealth of benefits. Embrace the journey of healthy eating, and watch as you and your family's health, happiness, and unity flourish.

Understanding Your Budget

Understanding your budget is a crucial first step toward achieving a healthy and satisfying diet for your family without breaking the bank. As a busy health professional, it can be easy to feel overwhelmed by the sheer number of financial responsibilities you face. However, taking the time to assess your budget can empower you to make informed decisions about your grocery shopping and meal planning. With a little effort, you can create a budget that allows for nutritious meals, ensuring that you eat well while still being mindful of your finances.

Start by tracking your current spending habits. Analyze your monthly expenses, focusing on food costs. This exercise will provide insight into where your money is going and highlight areas where you may be overspending. Are you frequently dining out or buying pre-packaged meals? Identifying these patterns can motivate you to shift your focus toward cooking at home, which is often healthier and more economical. Remember, every small change you make can lead to significant savings over time, allowing you to allocate more funds toward fresh ingredients.

Once you have a clear understanding of your spending, set realistic budget goals for your grocery shopping. Consider your family's dietary needs and preferences and determine how much you can comfortably spend each week or month. It's essential to strike a balance between maintaining a healthy diet and sticking to your financial plan. Look for ways to incorporate more whole foods, seasonal produce, and bulk items into your meals. These choices not only boost nutrition but can also help you stretch your budget further.

Meal planning is another effective strategy that can help you stay within your budget. By preparing a weekly menu and shopping list, you can avoid impulse buys and reduce food waste. Involve your children, if any, in this process; it can be a fun family activity that teaches them about healthy eating and budgeting. Choose recipes that use similar ingredients to maximize your purchases and minimize spoilage. This practice not only saves money but also simplifies your cooking process, making it easier to prepare nutritious meals during your busy week.

Lastly, remember that budgeting for healthy eating is a journey, not a destination. It may take time to find the right balance and adjust as time goes by with growth or changes. Celebrate your successes, no matter how small, and learn from any setbacks. With patience and persistence, you will develop a budget that works for you and supports a healthy lifestyle. Embrace this opportunity to create delicious, budget-friendly meals together that will nourish both your bodies and your family bond.

Meal Planning Basics

Meal planning is an essential skill for busy professionals and young families, if any, looking to eat healthy while staying within budget. It not only saves time during the week but also helps reduce food waste and encourages mindful eating. By dedicating a little time each week to plan meals, you can enjoy a variety of nutritious foods without the stress of last-minute decisions. With a few simple strategies, meal planning can become an enjoyable part of your routine that benefits everyone at the table.

Start by assessing your own needs and preferences. Consider dietary restrictions, favorite foods, and the number of meals you need to prepare each week. This will give you a clear foundation for your meal plan. Involve your children, if any, in the process by allowing them to suggest meals or help with the planning. This not only makes them more excited about the food you will eat but also teaches valuable skills in choosing and preparing healthy meals. Remember, the goal is to create a plan that works for your unique lifestyle.

Next, create a flexible yet structured meal plan. Aim for a balance of proteins, whole grains, fruits, and vegetables throughout the week. You might designate certain nights for specific types of meals, such as Meatless Mondays or Taco Tuesdays, which can help simplify decision-making. Incorporate leftovers into your plan to minimize cooking time and reduce waste. By preparing larger portions of certain meals, you can enjoy them again later in the week, making the most of your grocery budget and time spent in the kitchen.

Shopping smart is a vital part of successful meal planning. Make a grocery list based on your meal plan and stick to it to avoid impulse purchases. Look for sales and discounts on seasonal produce and staple items and consider buying in bulk for non-perishable goods. Don't shy away from generic brands, which can often provide the same quality at a lower price. Planning your meals around what's on sale not only saves money but also encourages creativity in the kitchen as you adapt your meals to what's available.

Finally, don't forget to be kind to yourself in the process. Meal planning is a journey, and it may take some time to find what works best. Embrace the learning curve and adjust as needed. Celebrate your successes, whether it's trying a new recipe or sticking to your plan for the week. With a little practice, meal planning can transform your approach to meals, making healthy eating both doable and enjoyable on a budget.

02

Chapter 2: Quick and Easy Breakfasts

Energizing Smoothies

Energizing smoothies are a fantastic way for busy medical professionals and young families to incorporate nutritious ingredients into their daily routines without breaking the bank. These delicious blends not only provide a quick meal option but also pack a powerful punch of vitamins, minerals, and energy boosting nutrients. With a little creativity and a few staple ingredients, you can whip up smoothies that everyone in the family will love, making healthy eating both enjoyable and economical.

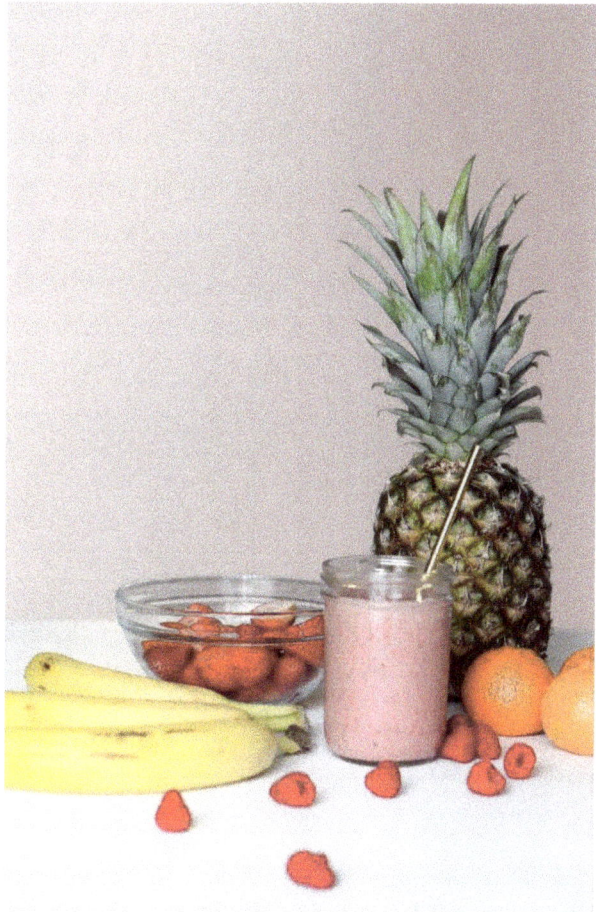

One of the best things about smoothies is their versatility. You can tailor them to suit your family's taste preferences and dietary needs while using seasonal fruits and vegetables to keep costs down. For instance, if you have a few ripe bananas sitting on your counter, blend them with some spinach, yogurt, and a splash of milk for a creamy, energizing treat. Frozen fruits are also a budget-friendly option that can add sweetness and nutrition to your drinks while keeping them chilled and refreshing. Experiment with different combinations and discover what your family enjoys most!

To maximize the health benefits of your smoothies, consider adding a handful of nutritious extras. Ingredients like oats, chia seeds, or nut butter not only enhance the flavor but also boost the fiber and protein content, keeping everyone satisfied for longer. These simple additions can turn a basic smoothie into a balanced meal perfect for breakfast or an afternoon snack. Plus, involving your kids in the smoothie-making process can be a fun way to teach them about healthy eating and encourage them to try new foods.

Preparing smoothies can be a time-saver for busy families. With just a few minutes in the morning or after school, you can create a nutritious drink that fuels your family's day. To streamline the process, consider prepping smoothie packs in advance. Portion out your favorite fruits and vegetables into freezer bags, so all you have to do is toss a bag into the blender with your liquid of choice. This not only saves time but also reduces food waste, as you can use up produce before it spoils.

Lastly, don't underestimate the power of smoothies to promote family bonding. Gather everyone in the kitchen and let each family member choose an ingredient to add to the mix. This collaborative effort can lead to new flavor combinations and create lasting memories in the process. By making energizing smoothies a regular part of your family's routine, you'll nurture a love for healthy eating while ensuring that your busy lifestyle aligns with your budget-friendly goals. Enjoy every sip and celebrate the healthy habits you're instilling in your family!

Healthy Egg Dishes

Eggs are a staple in many households, and for good reasons. They are not only affordable but also incredibly versatile, making them an ideal ingredient for busy families looking to whip up quick and healthy meals. Whether scrambled, poached, or baked, eggs can be transformed into a variety of dishes that are both nutritious and satisfying. Incorporating eggs into your family's diet can help you meet dietary needs without breaking the bank, ensuring that everyone is nourished and energized for the day ahead.

One of the simplest ways to enjoy eggs is through a classic scrambled dish. By adding vegetables like spinach, tomatoes, or bell peppers, you can boost the nutritional value while keeping preparation time to a minimum. A sprinkle of cheese or a dash of herbs can elevate the flavor without requiring elaborate cooking techniques. This dish can easily be tailored to suit your family's tastes and is perfect for breakfast, lunch, or even dinner. Plus, you can prepare it in just a few minutes, making it an ideal choice for those hectic mornings.

For families looking to pack in even more nutrition, consider making a frittata. This baked egg dish is not only hearty but also a fantastic way to use up leftover vegetables and proteins. Simply whisk together eggs, add your choice of ingredients, and let it bake in the oven. Frittatas are a great make ahead option, allowing you to slice and serve throughout the week, ensuring that healthy meals are always accessible. You can even serve it cold for a refreshing lunch option, making it a versatile addition to your recipe collection.

Another delightful option is to create egg muffins. These bite-sized treats are perfect for busy mornings and can be customized according to your family's preferences. By mixing eggs with diced vegetables, cheese, and cooked meats, you can make a batch of muffins that are protein-packed and easy to grab on the go. They freeze beautifully, so you can make a large batch and store them for those days when time is tight. This way, you won't have to sacrifice health for convenience, and your family can enjoy a nutritious breakfast any day of the week.

Lastly, don't overlook the beauty of simple boiled eggs. They are an excellent source of protein and can be prepared ahead of time for quick snacks or meal components. Boiled eggs can be cut up in salads, placed on whole grain toast, or simply enjoyed with a sprinkle of salt and pepper. They are portable and can be taken on outings, ensuring that your family has wholesome snacks readily available. By integrating healthy egg dishes into your weekly meal plan, you are not only providing essential nutrients but also fostering a love for healthy eating that will benefit your family in the long run.

03

Chapter 3: Wholesome Food on the Go

Smart Nutrition for Busy Medical Professionals: Easy, Healthy Meals & Snacks for Long Shifts

Medical professionals work long, demanding hours, often with limited breaks. When hunger strikes during a shift, it's tempting to reach for vending machine snacks or fast food. However, planning ahead with nutrient-dense, easily portable meals and snacks can sustain energy, improve focus, and support overall well-being.

Best Foods for Long, Stressful Workdays

The key to maintaining good nutrition on the job is choosing foods that are:
 Easy to prepare – Minimal effort before work
 Portable – No mess, no fuss
 Balanced – Protein, fiber, and healthy fats to sustain energy
 Delicious – Something you look forward to eating!

Great On-the-Go Snack Ideas

- Nuts & Seeds – Almonds, walnuts, pumpkin seeds (great for heart health and brain function)

- Greek Yogurt or Cottage Cheese – High-protein options that pair well with berries

- Hard-Boiled Eggs – A protein powerhouse, easy to peel and eat

- Hummus with Veggies – Carrot sticks, cucumber slices, or bell peppers for fiber and crunch

- String Cheese or Cheese Cubes – A calcium boost with satisfying protein

- Protein Bars – Look for low-sugar, whole-food-based options

- Apple Slices with Nut Butter – Provides fiber, healthy fat, and a natural energy boost

Easy-to-Pack Meals for Long Shifts

◈ Overnight Oats – Rolled oats, chia seeds, and berries soaked in almond milk, ready to grab and eat cold.

◈ Mason Jar Salads – Layer greens, protein (chicken, tuna, beans), veggies, and dressing at the bottom—shake and eat!

◈ Quinoa or Brown Rice Bowls – Combine with grilled chicken, roasted veggies, and avocado for a filling, balanced meal.

◈ Wraps & Roll-Ups – Whole grain tortillas filled with turkey, hummus, spinach, and shredded carrots for a quick bite.

◈ Soup in a Thermos – A warm, comforting meal with protein and veggies (chicken and lentil soup works great).

◈ Chia Pudding – Chia seeds soaked in almond or coconut milk with vanilla and cinnamon for a nutritious, ready-to-eat snack.

◈ Cold Pasta Salad – Whole wheat pasta with pesto, cherry tomatoes, olives, and feta for a fresh, Mediterranean-style meal.

Hydration & Energy Maintenance

- Infused Water - Add lemon, mint, or cucumber for a refreshing boost.

- Herbal Tea - Supports digestion and relaxation without caffeine crashes.

- Electrolyte-Rich Drinks - Coconut water or homemade electrolyte mixes help maintain balance during long hours.

By planning ahead and packing nutrient-rich meals and snacks, medical professionals can fuel their bodies for peak performance—without relying on processed, unhealthy options. A little preparation goes a long way in supporting overall health, energy, and mental clarity throughout the day.

Build-Your-Own Wraps

Wraps are a fantastic way to make mealtimes both fun and nutritious, especially for busy parents and young families. They offer endless possibilities for customization, allowing each family member to tailor their meal to their taste. This flexibility not only makes wraps a hit with kids but also helps parents stretch their grocery budgets while ensuring everyone eats healthy. By incorporating a variety of ingredients, you can create delicious wraps that are quick to prepare and packed with essential nutrients.

Start by choosing a base for your wrap. Whole grain tortillas, lettuce leaves, or even flatbreads make excellent options. Whole grain tortillas provide fiber and complex carbohydrates, while lettuce wraps are a refreshing, low-calorie alternative. Flatbreads can add a different texture and flavor to your meal. Once you have your base, the fun begins! Gather fresh vegetables, proteins, and spreads that your family enjoys. Carrots, bell peppers, cucumbers, and spinach not only add crunch and color but also boost the nutritional value of your wraps.

Next, select your protein source. Options like grilled chicken, turkey slices, or canned beans are budget-friendly and easy to prepare. You can also consider plant-based proteins such as hummus, tofu, or chickpeas for a nutritious twist. Involving your children in choosing the proteins can make them more excited about what they're eating, transforming the meal into a fun family activity. Encourage them to pick their favorites, fostering a sense of ownership and encouraging healthy eating habits.

Don't forget to add delicious spreads and seasonings to enhance the flavor of your wraps. A smear of avocado, a dollop of yogurt, or a drizzle of your favorite dressing can take your wraps to the next level. These flavorful additions not only enhance taste but also provide healthy fats and probiotics that are good for digestion. Experiment with different combinations to keep meals interesting and encourage your family to try new flavors. You might discover a new favorite that everyone loves.

Finally, make wrap-building a family affair. Set up a "wrap bar" where each person can assemble their own creation. This not only makes mealtimes interactive but also allows everyone to eat what they enjoy. By involving kids in preparation, you teach them valuable kitchen skills and promote healthier eating habits. Plus, it's an excellent opportunity for quality family time amid busy schedules. With this build-up-your-own wrap approach, you can create quick, healthy meals that fit your budget and satisfy everyone's tastes.

Nutritious Salads

Nutritious salads are a fantastic way for busy parents to incorporate a wealth of nutrients into their family's diet without breaking the bank. They can be prepared quickly, often in under 30 minutes, and can serve as a main dish or a side. By utilizing seasonal vegetables, canned beans, and whole grains, you can create hearty salads that are both satisfying and nourishing. Plus, these meals can be customized to fit your family's preferences, making them a perfect solution for picky eaters.

When planning your salads, think about incorporating a variety of colors and textures. This not only makes the dish visually appealing but also ensures a range of vitamins and minerals. Start with a base of leafy greens such as spinach, kale, or romaine. Add colorful veggies like bell peppers, cherry tomatoes, and carrots for crunch. Don't forget to mix in some protein sources like grilled chicken, tofu, or beans, which can help keep everyone full longer, making it a balanced meal that supports active lifestyles.

For those nights when time is tight, consider preparing ingredients in advance. You can wash and chop vegetables on the weekend and store them in airtight containers in the fridge. This strategy saves time during the week and makes it easy to throw together a quick salad. You can also use leftover proteins from dinner the night before, reducing waste and adding more nutrients to your salad without extra cost.

Dressing your salad can be a fun opportunity to experiment with flavors. Instead of store-bought dressings, which can be high in sugar and preservatives, whip up a simple homemade version using olive oil, vinegar, and your family's favorite herbs and spices. Not only is it healthier, but it also allows you to control the ingredients and adjust the flavors to suit your tastes. Encourage your kids to get involved by letting them choose their favorite ingredients for dressing, making it a fun family activity.

Finally, remember that salads can be a great way to introduce new foods to your family's diet. Use them as a canvas to try out different grains like quinoa or farro, or add unexpected ingredients like nuts and seeds for added crunch and nutrition. By making salads a regular part of your meals, you not only promote healthy eating habits but also create opportunities for family bonding while enjoying delicious, homemade food together. Nutritious salads are not just meals, they're a celebration of health and happiness for busy families.

Leftover Makeovers

Transforming leftovers into delicious meals can be a game change for busy parents who want to save time and money in the kitchen. Instead of letting uneaten food languish in the fridge, think of it as an opportunity to create something new and exciting. The beauty of leftovers is that they are often more versatile than you might think. With just a little creativity, you can turn last night's dinner into a brand-new family favorite in no time.

One of the simplest ways to revamp leftovers is by incorporating them into stir-fries. If you have extra vegetables, grains, or proteins from last night's meal, toss them into a hot skillet with some soy sauce or your favorite seasoning. This not only helps you clear out the fridge but also allows you to create a colorful and nutritious dish that your kids will love. Add some fresh herbs or a sprinkle of nuts for an extra crunch and a boost in flavor. Your family will be amazed at how delightful a simple stir-fry can be, and you'll feel great about reducing food waste.

Another fantastic way to give leftovers a new life is by turning them into wraps or sandwiches. Leftover roasted chicken, turkey, or even grilled veggies can be piled onto whole grain wraps with fresh greens, hummus, or yogurt-based dressing. Kids enjoy the fun of eating with their hands, and wraps are an excellent vehicle for sneaking in those leftover veggies. This option is quick to prepare and allows everyone to customize their meal to their liking. Plus, it's a great way to introduce new ingredients in a familiar format.

Casseroles are also a wonderful solution for leftover makeovers. Gather whatever proteins, grains, or vegetables you have on hand and combine them in a baking dish with a simple sauce or broth. Top with cheese or breadcrumbs and bake until bubbly. Casseroles are forgiving and adaptable, making it easy to use what you have without needing a specific recipe. This not only saves time but also makes for a cozy family meal that can be enjoyed for days, meaning more time for family activities and less time spent cooking.

Lastly, don't underestimate the power of soups and smoothies in utilizing leftovers. If you have vegetables that are nearing their end, throw them into a pot with some broth, seasonings, and any leftover grains you have for a hearty soup. For fruits, blend them into a smoothie with yogurt or milk for a refreshing snack or breakfast. These options are not only budget-friendly but also promote healthy eating habits within your family. Engaging your kids in the kitchen to help with these transformations can also turn meal prep into a fun family activity, reinforcing the importance of reducing waste and making the most of every ingredient.

04

Chapter 4:
Simple and
Satisfying Dinners

One-Pan Meals

One-pan meals are a lifesaver for busy parents navigating the hectic schedules of family life. With only one dish to clean, these meals simplify dinner prep and allow you to focus more on spending quality time with your loved ones. The beauty of one-pan meals lies not only in their ease but also in their versatility. You can combine various ingredients, from proteins and vegetables to grains, all in a single baking dish or skillet. This means you and your family can whip up nutritious dinners without the hassle of multiple pots and pans, making it a win-win for both your time and your kitchen.

Creating delicious one-pan meals doesn't require elaborate recipes or expensive ingredients. In fact, many of the components can be sourced from your pantry or local grocery store at budget-friendly prices. Staples like rice, pasta, or quinoa serve as the perfect base, while seasonal vegetables add freshness and flavor. By incorporating affordable proteins such as beans, eggs, or chicken thighs, you can easily create a filling and healthy meal that won't break the bank. With a little creativity, you'll find that a simple combination of ingredients can turn into a satisfying dish that the whole family will enjoy.

One of the most appealing aspects of one-pan meals is the time they save. After a long day of work, school, and activities, the last thing you want is to spend hours in the kitchen. Most one-pan recipes can be prepared in 30 minutes or less. With minimal prep work, you can throw everything together and let the oven or stovetop do the heavy lifting. This allows you to spend more time with your family, whether it's sharing stories from the day over dinner or enjoying a game night afterward. Embracing one-pan meals can help shift the focus from cooking to connecting.

Another advantage of one-pan meals is the opportunity to involve your children in the cooking process. Kids can help wash vegetables, measure ingredients, or even mix everything together. This not only teaches them valuable kitchen skills but also fosters a sense of responsibility and teamwork. When children are part of the cooking experience, they are often more willing to try new foods and appreciate the effort that goes into preparing meals. It's a great way to instill healthy eating habits and create lasting memories in the kitchen together.

Lastly, one-pan meals offer a fantastic way to embrace leftovers. Cooking in bulk means you can enjoy a delicious dinner today and have a ready-made lunch for tomorrow. Many one-pan dishes taste even better the next day as the flavors meld together. This not only contributes to a more sustainable approach to meal planning but also reduces food waste, making it a smart choice for budget-conscious families. With a little planning, you can transform your mealtime routine, ensuring that each dinner is quick, healthy, and enjoyable for the entire family.

Slow Cooker Comforts

Slow cookers are a game-changer for busy families, providing a simple solution to the daily dilemma of dinner preparation. With just a little planning, you can transform affordable ingredients into hearty meals that nourish both body and soul. The beauty of slow cooking lies in its ability to create complex flavors with minimal effort, allowing you to come home to a warm, inviting meal after a long day of work, school, and activities.

Embracing the slow cooker means you can spend less time in the kitchen and more time enjoying precious moments with your loved ones.

One of the most appealing aspects of slow cooking is its versatility. You can prepare a wide range of dishes, from savory stews and soups to tender roasts and flavorful casseroles. Budget-friendly cuts of meat, like chicken thighs or beef chuck, become incredibly tender when simmered for hours. You can also incorporate inexpensive vegetables, legumes, and grains, turning basic ingredients into satisfying meals that everyone will love. This approach not only keeps your grocery bills in check but also allows you to experiment with seasonal produce, making your meals both healthy and varied.

Moreover, cooking slow is an excellent way to sneak in more nutrition for your family. By starting with a base of vegetables, beans, or whole grains, you can create a wholesome foundation for your meals. Adding spices and herbs can elevate the flavors while providing various health benefits. For example, turmeric and ginger can introduce anti-inflammatory properties, while garlic and onions add both taste and important nutrients. The slow cooker allows these flavors to meld beautifully, resulting in dishes that are not only comforting but also packed with goodness.

Another advantage of slow cooking is the convenience it offers. Preparing a meal in the morning before heading out for the day means you can set it and forget it, freeing up your evenings for family time. Many slow cooker recipes require minimal prep work, allowing you to chop a few vegetables and throw everything into the pot. With a little creativity, you can even turn leftovers into new meals, reducing food waste and making the most of your budget. This flexibility is particularly helpful for busy parents juggling work, school schedules, and extracurricular activities.

As you venture into the world of slow cooker comforts, remember that the key is to embrace the process. Start with tried-and-true recipes, then gradually make them your own by adding your family's favorite ingredients or adjusting seasonings to suit your tastes. The joy of slow cooking is not just in the final dish but in the experience of creating meals that bring your family together. With each delicious creation, you'll not only nourish your family's bodies but also strengthen the bonds that make your house a home.

Quick Stir-Fry Options

Quick stir-fry options are a lifesaver for busy professional parents looking to prepare nutritious meals without spending hours in the kitchen. With just a few fresh ingredients and a hot pan, you can whip up a delicious dish that the whole family will love. Stir-frying allows for a variety of flavors and textures, making it an excellent choice for pleasing picky eaters while ensuring everyone gets a healthy dose of vegetables. Plus, it's an ideal way to use up any leftover ingredients you have on hand, minimizing waste and maximizing your grocery budget.

One of the simplest stir-fry options is a classic vegetable stir-fry. Gather whatever vegetables you have, broccoli, bell peppers, carrots, or snap peas work wonderfully. Toss them in a hot skillet with a splash of oil and your favorite seasonings, such as soy sauce or garlic. In just a matter of minutes, you'll have a colorful and vibrant dish. To make it more filling, consider adding a protein source like chicken, tofu, or shrimp. This flexibility means you can create a new dish each time based on what's available in your fridge.

For families with young children, a chicken and broccoli stir-fry can be a hit. Simply chop the chicken into bite-sized pieces and sauté them until golden brown. Add flavor in florets of broccoli and a splash of low-sodium soy sauce for flavor. This dish not only provides a balanced meal but also encourages kids to enjoy greens without fuss. Serve it over brown rice or quinoa for an extra boost of fiber, making it a wholesome dinner that supports healthy growth and development.

If time is of the essence, consider preparing a one-pan stir-fry. Using pre-cut vegetables or frozen stir-fry mixes can save valuable prep time. Heat a pan, throw in the protein of your choice, and add the vegetables directly. Season with a mix of ginger, garlic, and a hint of sesame oil for an authentic taste. This method keeps cleanup to a minimum, allowing you to spend more time with your family rather than washing dishes, which is a win for busy parents.

Lastly, don't forget the power of creativity in your stir-fry adventures. Experiment with different sauces, such as teriyaki or sweet and sour, to keep things exciting. You can also introduce whole grains like farro or barley instead of white rice for added nutrition. Stir-frying is not just about speed; it's also about variety and flavor. By involving your children in the cooking process, you can teach them valuable kitchen skills while encouraging them to try new foods. With these quick stir-fry options, healthy eating can be both delicious and achievable for busy families on a budget.

05

Chapter 5: Affordable Snacks for Busy Professionals and family

Homemade Energy Bites

Homemade energy bites are a fantastic solution for busy professionals looking to provide healthy snacks without breaking the bank. These no-bake treats are not only easy to prepare but also packed with nutrients that can fuel your family's day. With a few simple ingredients, you can whip up a variety of flavors that cater to your family's tastes, making snack time both enjoyable and nutritious. Investing a little time in the kitchen can yield delicious results that keep your family energized and satisfied.

One of the best aspects of energy bites is their versatility. You can customize them according to what you have on hand or what your family prefers. Basic recipes typically include oats, nut butter, and honey, but feel free to add extras like chocolate chips, dried fruits, seeds, or spices. This flexibility allows you to use up staples, reducing food waste and saving money. The kids can even join in the fun, mixing and rolling the bites into balls, which makes for a fun family activity that encourages healthy habits.

Not only are homemade energy bites budget-friendly, but they also allow you to control the ingredients, ensuring that your family is consuming wholesome, natural foods. Store-bought snacks often contain hidden sugars and preservatives, but when you make energy bites at home, you can opt for healthier alternatives. Choosing natural sweeteners, whole grains, and healthy fats means you are nourishing your family with every bite. Plus, knowing what goes into your snacks can give you peace of mind as a parent.

To make the most of your energy bites, consider preparing a large batch at the beginning of the week. Store them in the refrigerator or freezer for quick access during busy days. This way, when hunger strikes, you have a healthy option ready to go, eliminating the temptation of more processed snacks. These bites are perfect for after-school snacks, pre-workout boosts, or even a quick energy lift during a hectic day of work and errands. With a little planning, you can ensure you and your family has nutritious options readily available.

Incorporating homemade energy bites into your family's routine is an excellent step toward healthier eating without the stress of complicated recipes or high costs. Embrace the joy of creating these simple snacks together, and watch as your children develop a taste for nutritious foods.

By making energy bites a staple in your kitchen, you'll not only save money but also promote a lifestyle of healthy eating that your family will appreciate. Enjoy the process, experiment with flavors, and most importantly, have fun as you embark on this delicious journey together!

Fresh Fruit and Veggie Packs

Fresh fruit and veggie packs are an excellent way for busy professionals to ensure their families are getting the nutrients they need without spending hours in the kitchen. These packs are not only easy to prepare but also budget friendly, making them an ideal choice for families looking to eat healthily without breaking the bank. By incorporating a variety of colorful fruits and vegetables, you can create visually appealing snacks that excite kids and encourage them to make healthier choices.

Creating fresh fruit and veggie packs is a simple process that requires minimal time and effort. Start by selecting seasonal fruits and vegetables, as they tend to be more affordable and flavorful. Carrots, cucumbers, bell peppers, strawberries, and apples are popular options that are often well received by children. Spend a little time washing, cutting, and packaging these items into individual servings. By preparing them in advance, you can easily grab a pack on the go, ensuring that healthy snacks are always within reach.

Involving your children in the creation of these packs can make healthy eating even more enjoyable. Allow them to choose their favorite fruits and vegetables from the grocery store and participate in the preparation process. This not only teaches them about healthy eating but also gives them a sense of ownership over their food choices. When kids are involved, they're more likely to eat what they've helped create, making meal and snack times a pleasant experience for the whole family.

To add a fun twist to fresh fruit and veggie packs, consider including simple dips or spreads. Hummus, yogurt, or nut butter can enhance the appeal of raw vegetables and fruits, making them more enticing for young eaters. These additions can also provide extra protein and healthy fats, contributing to a well-rounded snack. By experimenting with different dips, you can keep things interesting and cater to your family's tastes while still prioritizing health.

In summary, fresh fruit and veggie packs are a practical solution for busy families striving to maintain healthy eating habits on a budget. They are quick to prepare, can be customized to suit individual preferences, and offer a delightful way to introduce more fruits and vegetables into your family's diet. By making these packs a regular part of your routine, you are setting your family up for a lifetime of healthy eating habits that are both enjoyable and sustainable.

Natural Nut Butter Delights

Natural Nut Butter Delights are a fantastic way to incorporate nutritious ingredients into your family's diet while keeping meals exciting and delicious. Nut butters (without added unhealthy fats), whether almond, peanut, or cashew, are packed with protein, healthy fats, and essential vitamins that support growth and development in children. The good news is that they are also incredibly versatile and can be used in a variety of recipes that are both quick to prepare and budget-friendly. With a little creativity, these delightful spreads can transform everyday snacks and meals into healthy favorites.

One of the simplest ways to enjoy natural nut butter is by spreading them on whole-grain bread or rice cakes. This classic combination provides a satisfying crunch and is perfect for a quick breakfast or after-school snack. To elevate the flavor and nutrition, consider topping it with sliced bananas, strawberries, or a sprinkle of cinnamon. These additions not only enhance the taste but also introduce extra vitamins and minerals to your family's diet. Plus, your kids will love the fun colors and textures, making mealtimes a visually appealing experience.

Natural nut butters can also shine smoothies, adding creaminess and a nutritional boost. Blend a tablespoon or two of your favorite nut butter with bananas, spinach, yogurt, and a splash of milk for a quick breakfast that keeps everyone full and energized. This is an excellent way to sneak in some greens without your kids even noticing! You can also experiment with different flavored combinations, such as chocolate protein powder with peanut butter or mixed berries with almond butter, to keep things interesting and cater to your family's preferences.

For those busy evenings when you need a quick dinner solution, nut butter can be transformed into delicious sauces. A simple peanut sauce made with natural peanut butter, soy sauce, and a splash of vinegar can elevate stir-fried vegetables and noodles into a hearty family meal. This sauce is not only easy to whip up, but it also allows you to get creative with whatever veggies and proteins you have on hand, ensuring that you stay within budget while providing a nutritious meal that the whole family will enjoy.

Lastly, don't overlook the power of natural nut butter with no added fats in baking. It can be a fantastic substitute for butter or oil in many recipes, reducing the overall fat content while still keeping treats moist and flavorful. Consider making natural nut butter cookies, energy balls, or even incorporating it into oatmeal for a wholesome breakfast treat. These recipes are not only budget-friendly but also allow you to involve your children in the kitchen, teaching them valuable cooking skills while creating delicious memories together. Natural Nut Butter Delights can easily become a staple in your family's healthy eating journey, proving that nutritious food doesn't have to be boring or expensive.

06

Chapter 6:
Family Friendly
Desserts

Healthy Fruit-Based Treats

Healthy Fruit-Based Treats can be a delightful way to introduce nutritious snacks into your family's routine without breaking the bank. Busy parents often struggle to find quick and healthy options that appeal to children, but fruit provides a versatile base for delicious treats that everyone will love. By incorporating simple, fresh ingredients, you can create satisfying snacks that not only taste great but also contribute to your family's overall wellness.

One of the easiest ways to enjoy fruit is by making homemade fruit popsicles. All you need are some fresh fruits, like bananas, strawberries, or peaches, and a blender. Combine your chosen fruits with a bit of yogurt or juice, pour the mixture into popsicle molds, and freeze. In just a few hours, you will have a refreshing treat that's perfect for hot days. This is a fantastic way to encourage your kids to eat more fruit while having fun creating their own flavors.

Another simple idea is to whip up a fruit salad that can double as a dessert. Choose a variety of colorful fruits, such as apples, oranges, blueberries, and grapes. Let your kids help with the preparation by washing and cutting the fruit, making them more excited to eat what they've helped to create. You can enhance this dish with a sprinkle of cinnamon or a drizzle of honey for added taste. This budget-friendly treat is not only visually appealing but also packed with vitamins and minerals.

If you're looking for a more filling snack, consider making fruit and nut energy balls. Combining oats, nut butter, and dried fruits like raisins or apricots, these bites are easy to prepare and provide a nutritious energy boost for busy days. Simply mix the ingredients in a bowl, roll them into small balls, and refrigerate. These treats can be made in bulk and stored for a quick grab-and-go option that keeps your family fueled throughout the day.

Lastly, don't forget about the classic banana ice cream, also known as "nice cream." Simply freeze ripe bananas, then blend them until smooth for a creamy, dairy-free dessert that feels indulgent without guilt. You can add cocoa powder, peanut butter, or a splash of vanilla extract for variety. This is a wonderful way to use overripe bananas and turn them into a delightful treat that kids will ask for again and again. By making these healthy fruit-based treats a regular part of your family's snack rotation, you can instill healthy eating habits while enjoying delicious and budget-friendly options together.

Guilt-Free Baking Ideas

Guilt-free baking can be a delightful way to engage the whole family while keeping health and budget in mind. With busy schedules, it can be tempting to reach for store-bought treats that may not align with your family's health goals. However, with a little creativity and some simple swaps, you can whip up delicious, homemade goodies that everyone will love without breaking the bank.

Start with wholesome ingredients that provide nutritional benefits without sacrificing flavor. Instead of refined sugars, consider using natural sweeteners like honey or maple syrup in moderation. Incorporating whole grains, such as whole wheat flour or oats, can add fiber and nutrients to your baked goods. For example, a simple oatmeal cookie recipe can be transformed into a healthier version by using mashed bananas or unsweetened applesauce to replace some of the fat and sugar. This not only cuts calories but also adds moisture and flavor, making the cookies a hit with kids.

Another fantastic idea is to experiment with adding fruits and vegetables into your baking. Carrot muffins, zucchini bread, or banana pancakes can become family favorites while sneaking in those essential nutrients. You can also create a fun family activity by letting your kids help mix in the ingredients. This not only teaches them about healthy eating but also allows them to take ownership of their meals, making them more likely to enjoy what they've helped create.

Consider portion control when baking to keep those treats from becoming overly indulgent. Mini muffins or bite-sized brownies can satisfy a sweet tooth without overdoing it. You can even make a batch of healthy energy bites using oats, natural nut butter, and a touch of honey for a quick snack that's easy to grab on the go. These small adjustments can help instill healthy habits in your children while still celebrating the joys of baking together.

Lastly, remember that healthy baking doesn't have to be complicated or time-consuming. Many recipes can be whipped up in under thirty minutes, making them perfect for busy families. With a little planning, you can stock your pantry with essential ingredients and have fun baking sessions that fit seamlessly into your routine. Embrace the joy of creating delicious treats that everyone can enjoy, and watch as your family develops a love for healthy, homemade snacks.

Frozen Yogurt Pops

Frozen yogurt pops are a delightful and nutritious treat that busy parents can easily whip up at home, making them a perfect addition to your family's healthy eating routine. These pops are not only simple to prepare but also budget-friendly, allowing you to make delicious snacks without breaking the bank. With just a few ingredients and minimal prep time, you can create a variety of flavors that your kids will love, all while sneaking in some extra nutrition.

To make frozen yogurt pops, start with a base of plain yogurt, which is rich in protein and probiotics. You can use any type of yogurt your family enjoys, whether it's low-fat, Greek, or non-dairy alternatives. The beauty of this recipe is its versatility; you can mix in fresh fruits, a drizzle of honey, or even a splash of vanilla extract to enhance the flavor. Involve your children in the process by letting them choose their favorite fruits or toppings, turning the preparation into a fun family activity.

One of the best things about frozen yogurt pops is the opportunity they present for creativity. Try blending yogurt with fruits like strawberries, bananas, or mangoes for a refreshing taste. You can even layer different fruit purees to create visually appealing pops that will excite your kids. For added texture, consider mixing in granola or crushed nuts before freezing. This not only adds crunch but also makes the pop more filling, providing a satisfying snack option that keeps hunger at bay.

When it comes to freezing, simple molds are all you need. You can find affordable silicone molds in various shapes and sizes or even repurpose small paper cups and popsicle sticks. Pour the yogurt mixture into the molds, insert sticks, and place them in the freezer for a few hours. The waiting time is well worth it, as your family will be rewarded with delicious homemade frozen treats that are free from artificial ingredients and added sugars.

These frozen yogurt pops make for perfect after-school snacks, summer treats, or even a healthy dessert option. They are easy to store in the freezer, allowing you to always have a nutritious snack on hand. With just a little planning, you can ensure that you and your family enjoys sweet, healthy treats that fit into your budget. So, gather your ingredients, get creative in the kitchen, and watch your children delight in these wholesome frozen yogurt pops that combine fun and nutrition in every bite.

07

Chapter 7:
Shopping Smart

Creating a Budget-Friendly Grocery List

Creating a budget-friendly grocery list is an essential step for busy parents and young families striving to maintain healthy eating habits while keeping expenses in check. The key to successful grocery shopping lies in preparation and planning. Start by assessing your family's dietary needs and preferences. This not only helps in selecting nutritious options but also ensures that everyone in the family is satisfied and excited about mealtime. When you know what your family enjoys, you can create a targeted list that reduces impulse buys and keeps your shopping trips efficient.

Begin with your grocery planning by taking stock of what you already have in your pantry and refrigerator. This will prevent unnecessary purchases and help you utilize ingredients you may have forgotten about. Make a list of meals you plan to prepare for the week, focusing on recipes that use similar ingredients. This strategy not only minimizes waste but also allows you to buy in bulk, which can often save money. Remember, cooking in batches and using leftovers creatively can stretch your budget even further while providing nutritious meals for your family.

When it comes to actual grocery shopping, opt for seasonal produce. Seasonal fruits and vegetables are often more affordable and taste better. Additionally, consider visiting local farmers' markets or participating in community-supported agriculture (CSA) programs. These options can provide you with fresh, local produce at competitive prices while also supporting your community. Don't shy away from frozen fruits and vegetables as well; they are picked at peak ripeness and can be more budget-friendly than fresh options, particularly out of season.

Fiber is so Important

Fiber is essential for digestive health, blood sugar balance, and keeping your family full and satisfied between meals. There are two types of fiber— soluble and insoluble—both of which can be easily incorporated into baked goods and everyday recipes. Soluble fiber, found in oats, flaxseeds, and psyllium husk, helps slow digestion and support heart health by lowering cholesterol levels. Insoluble fiber, found in whole wheat, bran, nuts, and seeds, promotes regularity and gut health. Adding fiber to baked goods is simple—swap white flour for whole wheat or almond flour, mix in ground flaxseeds or chia seeds, or add a spoonful of psyllium husk to pancakes, muffins, and bread. Even a sprinkle of prebiotic-rich resistant starch from green banana flour or potato starch can boost digestion and promote a healthy gut microbiome.

Reading Food Labels Is Critical

Reading food labels is one of the most powerful ways to protect your family's health from harmful ingredients hidden in processed foods. Many packaged foods contain artificial additives, unhealthy fats, and genetically modified organisms (GMOs) that can negatively impact health. To make informed choices, look for short ingredient lists with recognizable, whole-food ingredients. Avoid harmful additives such as high-fructose corn syrup, hydrogenated oils (trans fats), artificial colors (like Red 40 and Yellow 5), monosodium glutamate (MSG), and artificial sweeteners such as aspartame and sucralose. Many processed foods also contain genetically modified soy, corn, and canola, which may contribute to inflammation and other health concerns. Choosing organic, non-GMO, and minimally processed foods ensures that you are providing your family with the healthiest options while avoiding harmful chemicals and unnecessary additives.

As you build your grocery list, (see the resource page in the back) prioritize whole foods over processed items. Foods like grains, beans, and legumes are not only cost-effective but also incredibly nutritious. Incorporating these staples into your meals can help stretch your budget while providing your family with essential nutrients. Look for sales or discounts on these items, and consider purchasing generic brands, which often offer the same quality as name brands at a lower price. This small change can lead to significant savings over time.

Lastly, always be mindful of your grocery budget while shopping. Set a specific amount you aim to spend each week and stick to it. If you find yourself tempted by a non-essential item, ask yourself if it fits into your meal plan or if it aligns with your family's health goals. By staying focused and disciplined, you can create a grocery list that not only supports a healthy lifestyle but also respects your budget. With the right planning and mindful choices and reading the ingredient labels, healthy eating on a budget can be both achievable and enjoyable for your family.

Fiber is essential for digestive health, blood sugar balance, and keeping your family full and satisfied between meals. There are two types of fiber—soluble and insoluble—both of which can be easily incorporated into baked goods and everyday recipes. Soluble fiber, found in oats, flaxseeds, and psyllium husk, helps slow digestion and support heart health by lowering cholesterol levels. Insoluble fiber, found in whole wheat, bran, nuts, and seeds, promotes regularity and gut health. Adding fiber to baked goods is simple—swap white flour for whole wheat or almond flour, mix in ground flaxseeds or chia seeds, or add a spoonful of psyllium husk to pancakes, muffins, and bread. Even a sprinkle of prebiotic-rich resistant starch from green banana flour or potato starch can boost digestion and promote a healthy gut microbiome.

Reading food labels is one of the most powerful ways to protect your family's health from harmful ingredients hidden in processed foods. Many packaged foods contain artificial additives, unhealthy fats, and genetically modified organisms (GMOs) that can negatively impact health. To make informed choices, look for short ingredient lists with recognizable, whole-food ingredients. Avoid harmful additives such as high-fructose corn syrup, hydrogenated oils (trans fats), artificial colors (like Red 40 and Yellow 5), monosodium glutamate (MSG), and artificial sweeteners such as aspartame and sucralose. Many processed foods also contain genetically modified soy, corn, and canola, which may contribute to inflammation and other health concerns. Choosing organic, non-GMO, and minimally processed foods ensures that you are providing your family with the healthiest options while avoiding harmful chemicals and unnecessary additives.

Seasonal Produce and Sales

Incorporating seasonal produce into your family's meals not only enhances the flavor and nutritional value of your dishes but also supports your budget. When fruits and vegetables are in season, they are often more affordable and abundant, allowing you to enjoy fresh ingredients without breaking the bank. Busy parents can take advantage of local farmers' markets or grocery stores that highlight seasonal offerings. By making a habit of checking what's in season, you'll find that planning meals becomes easier and more enjoyable.

Understanding the seasonal produce in your area can empower you to create a diverse and colorful plate for your family. For instance, spring brings vibrant asparagus and sweet peas, summer is abundant with tomatoes and berries, while fall offers hearty squash and apples. Winter may seem limited, but root vegetables and hearty greens provide excellent options. By rotating these seasonal ingredients in your meals, you can keep your menu exciting, and your family engaged in trying new flavors and textures.

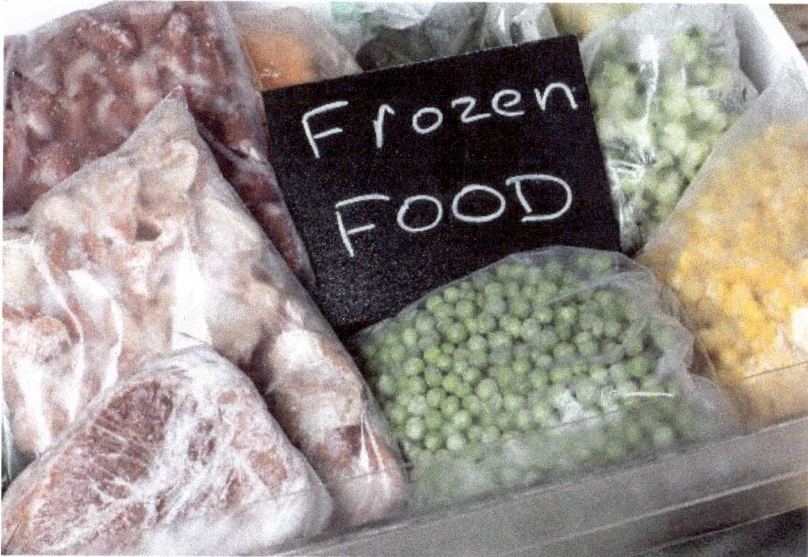

Planning your shopping around seasonal produce can lead to significant savings. Instead of purchasing out-of-season fruits and vegetables that often come with a higher price tag and lower quality, focus on what is currently available. Create a weekly meal plan that utilizes these ingredients, making sure to include a variety of colors and types for balanced nutrition. This approach not only helps you stay within your budget but also encourages healthier eating habits for your children, as they get to experience the full range of flavors that nature has to offer.

As you explore seasonal produce, consider involving your children in the process. Take them on a trip to the market, allowing them to pick out fruits and vegetables that catch their eye. This not only makes grocery shopping a fun adventure but also fosters a sense of ownership in their meals.

Encourage them to help you prepare dishes using these ingredients, teaching them valuable cooking skills while reinforcing the importance of healthy eating. When kids are part of the process, they are more likely to enjoy and appreciate the meals you create together.

Lastly, don't hesitate to experiment with your cooking! Seasonal produce can inspire creativity in the kitchen, leading to delightful discoveries. Try making a refreshing summer salad with ripe peaches or a comforting winter stew loaded with root vegetables. The possibilities are endless, and the excitement of trying new recipes can be a fantastic family bonding experience. Embrace the changes each season brings to your table, and watch as your family's appreciation for healthy, budget-friendly meals grows.

Bulk Buying Tips

When it comes to managing a busy household, bulk buying can be a game changer for both your budget and your family's health. By purchasing items in larger quantities, you can save money while ensuring you have nutritious ingredients on hand for your meals. Start by making a list of staples your family enjoys—think grains, legumes, canned goods, frozen vegetables, and healthy snacks. This will help you avoid impulse purchases and ensure you only buy what you will actually use. Remember, the goal is to fill your pantry with items that support your family's health and your budget.

Consider shopping at warehouse stores or joining a co-op to access bulk items. These venues often offer lower prices on larger quantities, which can lead to significant savings over time. If you're unsure whether your family can consume the amounts you buy, partner with friends or neighbors for group purchases. Sharing bulk items not only cuts costs but also fosters community connections. It's a win-win situation that allows you to enjoy the benefits of bulk buying without the fear of waste. **Note: Misfits Market and Hungry Harvest sell imperfect fruits and vegetables.** These companies deliver discounted produce to your door.

Storage is key when it comes to bulk purchasing. Make sure you have space in your pantry, freezer, and refrigerator to accommodate larger quantities. Invest in airtight containers to keep dry goods fresh and prevent spoilage. Label everything with purchase dates to keep track of what you have and ensure you use items before they go bad. For perishables, consider meal prepping or cooking in batches to make the most of your bulk buys. This way, you can freeze meals for busy nights, ensuring your family always has healthy options ready to go.

Don't forget to incorporate seasonal produce into your bulk buying strategy. When fruits and vegetables are in season, they are often available at lower prices. Buy in bulk and freeze or preserve them for later use, ensuring your family gets the benefits of fresh produce year-round. This not only enhances your meals but also encourages healthy eating habits in your children. They'll learn to appreciate the value of fresh foods while you save money at the same time.

Finally, maintain flexibility in your meal planning. When you have a variety of bulk items, you can easily adjust your meals based on what you have on hand. Use your inventory to create a rotating menu that incorporates different ingredients, ensuring your family enjoys diverse, healthy meals throughout the week. With a little creativity and planning, you can turn bulk buying into a fun and rewarding experience for your family, making healthy eating both budget-friendly and enjoyable.

08

Chapter 8:
Cooking Together as
a Family

Involving Kids in Meal Prep

Involving kids in meal prep can transform the kitchen into a fun and educational space while fostering healthy eating habits. When children participate in preparing their meals, they develop a sense of ownership over what they eat, making them more likely to try new foods. This engagement not only nurtures their culinary skills but also teaches valuable lessons about nutrition and the importance of healthy eating. Busy parents can take advantage of this opportunity to bond with their children and instill a positive attitude towards food from a young age.

One effective way to involve kids in meal prep is by assigning age-appropriate tasks. Younger children can help wash vegetables, tear lettuce, or measure out ingredients, while older kids can take on more complex responsibilities like chopping, stirring, or following recipes. By giving them specific roles, you empower them to contribute meaningfully to the cooking process. This sense of contribution boosts their confidence and makes mealtime more exciting for everyone involved. Remember to celebrate their efforts, no matter how small, to encourage a lifelong interest in cooking.

Planning meals together is another excellent strategy to involve kids in the kitchen. Set aside time each week to sit down as a family and discuss the upcoming meals. Let the kids share their favorite foods and help brainstorm healthy options. This collaborative approach not only makes them feel valued but also teaches them about meal planning and budgeting. When they take part in deciding what to eat, they are more likely to be enthusiastic about the meals you prepare together, which can ease the stress of mealtime battles.

Incorporating educational elements into meal prep can also enhance the experience. Use this time to teach your kids about different food groups, the nutritional value of ingredients, and how to read labels. You can even incorporate math skills by having them measure ingredients or calculate portion sizes. This holistic approach not only makes meal preparation a learning opportunity but also reinforces the idea that healthy eating is an essential part of a balanced lifestyle. The more they know, the more likely they are to make healthy choices independently.

Finally, creating a family cooking tradition can make meal prep something to look forward to. Dedicate one night a week as "Family Cooking Night," where everyone comes together to create a meal. This tradition can be a special time to bond, share stories, and enjoy each other's company amidst the hustle and bustle of daily life. As your children grow, they will carry these memories with them, and the skills they learn will serve them well in the future. By involving kids in meal prep, you are not only making eating healthy a family affair but also laying the foundation for a lifetime of positive food experiences.

Fun Cooking Challenges

Cooking can often feel like a chore, especially for busy parents juggling work, kids, and a myriad of daily tasks. However, introducing fun cooking challenges into your family routine can transform mealtime into an enjoyable and engaging experience. These challenges not only encourage creativity in the kitchen but also promote teamwork, making cooking a delightful bonding activity for your family.

One exciting idea is to host a themed cooking night. Choose a theme, such as Italian, Mexican, or even a color theme where all ingredients must be a specific color. Involve your children in the decision-making process and let them help with research on traditional dishes. This approach not only makes cooking fun but also allows kids to explore different cultures and cuisines, expanding their palates and appreciation for diverse foods—all without breaking the bank.

Another great challenge is a "mystery ingredient" contest. Each family member can select a healthy ingredient from the pantry or fridge that must be included in the meal. This could be anything from spinach to quinoa, and the challenge is to create a dish that highlights that ingredient. Encourage your kids to think outside the box and come up with recipes. This not only fosters creativity but also teaches children how to incorporate nutritious ingredients in delicious ways, ensuring that healthy eating becomes a family affair.

For those looking to save money while being adventurous, consider the "leftover makeover" challenge. Each week, pick a day dedicated to using up leftovers or pantry items that might otherwise go to waste. Let everyone in the family contribute by suggesting ideas for how to combine various leftovers into a new dish. This challenge promotes resourcefulness and teaches kids the importance of minimizing waste while also having fun experimenting with flavors and textures.

Lastly, a "cook-off" can be a thrilling way to inject some competition into your kitchen. Divide into teams and set a timer to create a healthy dish using a limited number of ingredients. Not only does this encourage quick thinking and teamwork, but it also allows kids to take ownership of their cooking skills. Celebrate everyone's efforts with a family taste test and award fun titles like "Best Presentation" or "Most Creative Flavor." These experiences will not only bring joy to your kitchen but will also create lasting memories and instill a love for healthy cooking in your children.

Making Mealtime a Family Event

Making mealtime a family event can transform the experience of eating together into one of joy and connection. For busy parents and young families, the challenge often lies in finding the time amidst hectic schedules. Embracing mealtimes as a family event doesn't require extensive planning or gourmet cooking; it simply takes a commitment to prioritize shared meals. By creating a welcoming atmosphere and involving everyone in the process, you can foster a sense of belonging and togetherness that strengthens family bonds.

One effective way to make mealtimes a family event is to involve your children in the preparation of meals. Tasks can be divided according to age, allowing younger children to wash vegetables while older ones can handle chopping or stirring. Not only does this teach valuable cooking skills, but it also makes children feel included and invested in the meal. As they help prepare the food, they become more likely to try new dishes and appreciate the effort that goes into creating a healthy meal for everyone.

Setting a designated mealtime can also encourage families to gather regularly. Whether it's breakfast, lunch, or dinner, having a specific time when everyone sits down to eat helps establish a routine. Consider making it a tradition to share stories from the day or to discuss something you're thankful for. This ritual can turn mealtime into a cherished moment where everyone feels heard and valued. It doesn't have to be a long discussion; even a few minutes of sharing can create a warm, family-centered atmosphere.

In addition to involving family members in meal prep and establishing a routine, you can enhance the mealtime experience by creating a pleasant dining environment. Simple touches, such as setting the table together, turning off distractions, and perhaps adding a tablecloth and even lighting a candle, can make meals feel special. Encouraging everyone to participate in this process, even in small ways, fosters a sense of ownership and pride in the family meal. Remember, the goal is not perfection but connection, so keep it light and enjoyable.

Finally, embracing the concept of mealtimes as a family event can have lasting benefits beyond just nutrition. It cultivates an environment where children learn the importance of healthy eating habits while also creating lasting memories. By making mealtime a priority, you're instilling values of togetherness, gratitude, and communication that will benefit your family for years to come. So, gather around the table, share a laugh, and enjoy the simple pleasure of nourishing your bodies and your relationships.

09

Chapter 9:
Staying Motivated

Setting Realistic Goals

Setting realistic goals is essential for busy parents and young families striving to maintain a healthy lifestyle while staying within budget. The first step in this journey is to identify what works best for your family's unique situation. Consider your daily schedule, the preferences of each family member, and the resources available to you. By taking an honest assessment of your circumstances, you can create achievable goals that fit into your life rather than overwhelm it. Remember, small changes can lead to significant improvements over time.

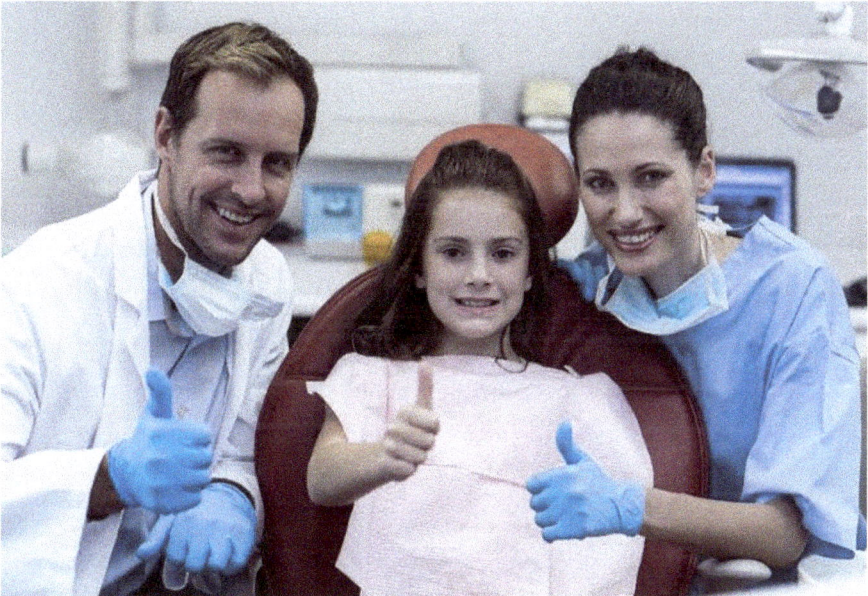

Next, focus on specific, measurable objectives that resonate with your family's needs. Instead of vague aspirations like "eat healthier," aim for concrete goals such as "include one serving of vegetables at dinner three times a week." This approach not only clarifies your intentions but also provides a tangible way to track progress. Celebrate small victories along the way, as they can boost motivation and encourage your family to stay committed to healthier eating habits without feeling deprived.

Involving the whole family in the goal-setting process can enhance buy-in and accountability. Take time to sit down together and discuss what healthy eating means to each of you. Encourage everyone to share ideas and preferences, making it a fun and engaging activity. When children feel included in planning meals and snacks, they are more likely to embrace these changes. Consider creating a family meal chart or a weekly cooking session to reinforce teamwork and make healthy eating a shared responsibility.

Flexibility is a vital component of setting realistic goals. Life with young children can be unpredictable, and rigid plans may lead to frustration. Instead, allow for adjustments based on your family's schedule and energy levels. If a planned healthy meal doesn't happen one night, don't be discouraged; simply move it to another evening or opt for a quick, nutritious alternative. Embracing flexibility will not only alleviate stress but also foster a positive approach to healthy eating that can adapt to your family's evolving needs.

Finally, remember that the journey to healthier eating is a marathon, not a sprint. Progress may be gradual, but every step counts. Keep your goals manageable and revisit them periodically to assess how they align with your family's lifestyle. As you achieve these goals, you'll likely find that healthy eating becomes more intuitive and enjoyable. By setting realistic expectations, you'll create a sustainable path toward better nutrition for your family, all while being mindful of your budget.

Celebrating Small Wins

Celebrating small wins is an essential part of the journey toward healthier eating, especially for busy parents and young families. In the whirlwind of daily activities, from school runs to work commitments, it's easy to overlook the little victories that pave the way for lasting change. Recognizing and celebrating small achievements can boost morale, (have you heard of using a red plate for celebrations?) can foster a positive mindset, and create a supportive atmosphere in your home. Whether it's managing to cook a nutritious meal on a particularly hectic night or getting the kids to try a new veggie, each win deserves acknowledgment.

One of the simplest ways to celebrate small wins is to create a family ritual. Consider setting aside a few minutes each week to reflect on what went well in your kitchen. Did you successfully prepare a healthy dinner within 30 minutes? Did everyone finish their servings of vegetables? Perhaps you managed to stick to your grocery budget while still picking up fresh produce. Sharing these moments as a family not only reinforces positive behavior but also instills a sense of accomplishment in everyone. These discussions can inspire even more healthy habits moving forward.

Another effective strategy is to incorporate fun rewards for achieving small goals. These rewards don't have to be extravagant; they can be as simple as a family night, a special dessert made together, or even a picnic in the living room. When your family hits a milestone—like cooking a healthy meal five times in a week, celebrate it! This not only rewards the effort but also encourages everyone to continue striving for more, creating a cycle of positivity and motivation in the kitchen.

Recognizing the importance of small wins can also help shift the focus from perfection to progress. For busy parents, it's easy to become overwhelmed by the quest for an ideal healthy lifestyle. Instead, celebrate the fact that you've chosen to prioritize nutrition, even if that means ordering a healthier takeout once a week rather than cooking every night. Each step taken towards healthier eating, no matter how small, is a step in the right direction. This mindset can alleviate pressure and create a more enjoyable experience for everyone involved.

In the end, it's the accumulation of these small victories that leads to significant changes in your family's eating habits. By celebrating each achievement, you cultivate a family culture that values health and wellness. These moments of triumph not only reinforce your commitment to healthier eating but also strengthen family bonds. So, take a moment to acknowledge what you've accomplished, big or small, and let that sense of achievement propel you forward on your journey to budget-friendly, healthy eating for your family.

Building Healthy Habits

Building healthy habits is essential for busy parents and young families striving to maintain a balanced lifestyle without breaking the bank. Establishing routines centered around nutritious eating can seem daunting, but with a few strategic approaches, it can become a seamless part of your family's daily life. By making small, manageable changes, you can foster an environment where healthy choices are the norm rather than the exception.

Start by involving the whole family in meal planning and preparation. This not only makes the process more enjoyable but also teaches children valuable skills and the importance of nutrition. Set aside a specific time each week to sit down together and brainstorm meal ideas. Encourage everyone to contribute to their favorite healthy dishes and make it a fun activity to explore new recipes. This collaboration can help create excitement around healthy eating and ensure that everyone feels included in the decision-making process.

When grocery shopping, stick to a list that prioritizes whole foods and seasonal produce to keep costs down while maximizing nutrition. Fresh fruits, vegetables, grains, and lean proteins are the building blocks of a healthy diet. If you involve your children in the shopping process, they can help select the items on the list, which can lead to a greater willingness to try new foods. Teaching kids about budgeting while shopping can turn the experience into a valuable lesson about healthy eating and financial responsibility.

Incorporating healthy snacks into your family's routine is another effective way to build good habits. Prepare a variety of quick and nutritious snack options, such as sliced fruits, yogurt, or homemade granola bars, and keep them readily accessible. This simple step can prevent impulse buying unhealthy snacks while also ensuring that your family has energy-boosting options on hand throughout the day. Encourage children to grab these healthy snacks when hunger strikes, reinforcing the idea that nutritious food is both delicious and convenient.

Lastly, make mealtime a family affair. Set aside time each day to sit down together for meals without distractions. This practice not only strengthens family bonds but also allows for meaningful conversations about the importance of healthy eating. As you share a meal, discuss the benefits of the foods you're enjoying, and highlight the positive effects of maintaining a balanced diet. By creating a supportive atmosphere around healthy eating, you set the stage for lifelong habits that will benefit your family for years to come.

10

Chapter 10:
Resources and Tools

Recommended Cookbooks and Blogs

When it comes to quick and healthy cooking for busy families, having the right resources can make all the difference. There is a wealth of cookbooks and blogs specifically tailored to help you navigate the challenges of preparing nutritious meals on a budget. These resources not only provide you with delicious recipes but also offer valuable tips on meal planning, shopping smart, and making the most of seasonal ingredients. Embracing these tools can empower you to create a positive cooking experience for your family, even on the busiest of days.

One highly recommended cookbook is "The Weekday Vegetarians" by Jenny Rosen Strach. This book focuses on simple, plant-based meals that are both satisfying and easy to prepare. With its emphasis on family-friendly recipes, it encourages you to incorporate more vegetables into your diet without sacrificing flavor. Each recipe is designed to be made in thirty minutes or less, making it perfect for those chaotic weeknights when time is of the essence. Plus, the beautiful photography and relatable anecdotes make cooking feel like a joyful experience rather than a chore.

Another fantastic resource is the blog "Budget Bytes" by Beth Moncel. This blog is dedicated to providing budget-friendly recipes that don't compromise on taste or nutrition. Beth shares her cooking journey on a tight budget and provides insights into meal prep and grocery shopping with money-saving tips. Each recipe includes a cost breakdown, allowing you to see exactly how much you're spending on each meal. The practical approach and accessibility of her recipes make it easy for busy parents to whip up delicious meals without breaking the bank.

For those who prefer a more hands-on approach, "The Instant Pot Electric Pressure Cooker Cookbook" by Laurel Randolph is an excellent choice. This cookbook offers a variety of quick and healthy recipes that can be made in an Instant Pot, a game-changer for busy families. With the ability to prepare meals in a fraction of the time, you can enjoy wholesome dishes without the long wait. Each recipe is designed to maximize flavor while keeping preparation time to a minimum, allowing you to spend more time with your family and less time in the kitchen.

Finally, "The Healthy Meal Prep Cookbook" by Toby Amador provides a comprehensive guide to meal prepping, which can be a lifesaver for busy families. This resource is filled with nutritious recipes that can be prepared in advance, ensuring you always have a healthy option on hand. The book emphasizes the importance of planning and organization, teaching you how to streamline your cooking process while staying within your budget. With its practical advice and straightforward recipes, you'll find it easier to create delicious meals that your family will love while keeping your finances in check. By utilizing these cookbooks and blogs, you can confidently tackle the challenge of healthy eating for your family, making mealtimes enjoyable and stress-free.

Kitchen Gadgets for Quick Cooking

In the fast-paced world of busy parents and young families, the kitchen can often feel like a battleground where time is a precious commodity. Thankfully, the right kitchen gadgets can transform this space into a haven of efficiency, making quick cooking not only possible but enjoyable. Investing in a few key tools can significantly cut down on preparation time and help you whip up healthy meals without breaking the bank. Let's explore some essential kitchen gadgets that will support your goal of budget-friendly, nutritious cooking.

One of the standout gadgets for quick cooking is the slow cooker. This versatile appliance allows you to prepare meals in advance, freeing up valuable time during the week. Simply toss your ingredients in the morning, set it to cook, and return home to a warm, ready-to-eat meal. Whether it's a hearty stew or a vegetable-packed chili, slow cookers can help you create delicious dishes that often taste even better the next day. Plus, many slow cooker recipes use budget-friendly ingredients, making them perfect for families watching their spending.

An immersion blender is another fantastic tool that can save you time and effort in the kitchen. This handheld device allows you to puree soups directly in the pot, blend smoothies in seconds, or create homemade sauces without the hassle of transferring ingredients to a traditional blender. With an immersion blender, you can easily incorporate more fruits and vegetables into your family's diet, promoting healthy eating without the mess of extra dishes. It's a compact gadget that packs a punch when it comes to quick meal preparation.

Pressure cookers, particularly electric models, have gained popularity for a good reason. They significantly reduce cooking times, allowing you to prepare meals that would typically take hours to cook in a fraction of the time. Whether you're cooking grains, beans, or tough cuts of meat, a pressure cooker can make them tender and flavorful in a short period. This efficiency not only saves time but also energy, making it an eco-friendly choice for the conscious family. Additionally, many pressure cooker recipes are designed to be budget-friendly, helping you make the most of your grocery budget.

Finally, don't underestimate the power of a good set of kitchen knives. Investing in quality knives can make food prep quicker and more enjoyable. A sharp chef's knife, a paring knife, and a bread knife are essentials that can help you chop, slice, and dice with ease. When your tools are effective, meal prep becomes less of a chore and more of a fun family activity. Encourage your children to join in the process, teaching them valuable skills while making healthy meals together.

By incorporating these kitchen gadgets into your cooking routine, you can streamline your meal preparation and focus on what truly matters: spending quality time with your family. Quick cooking doesn't have to sacrifice nutrition or taste, and with a little help from the right tools, you can create budget-friendly meals that everyone will love. Embrace these gadgets as allies in your quest for healthy eating and enjoy the delicious results that come from your kitchen adventures.

Apps for Meal Planning and Budgeting

In today's fast-paced world, busy parents are often juggling multiple responsibilities, making meal planning and budgeting challenging. Fortunately, technology has come to the rescue with various apps designed specifically for families looking to eat healthy without breaking the bank. These tools can streamline the meal planning process, allowing you to focus on what truly matters: spending quality time with your loved ones while enjoying nutritious meals.

Meal planning apps like Mealtime and Plan to Eat can significantly simplify your weekly meal prep. They enable you to create personalized meal plans based on your family's preferences and dietary needs. With user-friendly interfaces, these apps allow you to select recipes, generate shopping lists, and even schedule meals for the week. By dedicating just a few minutes each week to planning, you can save time and reduce the stress of lastminute cooking, while ensuring that your family eats healthily and deliciously.

Budgeting apps such as Mint or YNAB (You Need A Budget) can work hand in-hand with your meal planning efforts. These tools help you track your grocery spending and set budget limits, making it easier to stick to your financial goals. By monitoring your expenses, you can identify areas where you might be overspending and redirect those funds toward healthier food choices. The combination of meal planning and budgeting not only promotes healthier eating habits but also fosters financial awareness in your family.

Another great resource is grocery store apps that often provide digital coupons and weekly ads, allowing you to make the most of your budget. Many stores have their own apps that feature personalized deals and discounts based on your shopping history. By leveraging these savings, you can buy fresh ingredients for your meal plans without feeling guilty about the cost. This approach not only ensures that you are providing your family with wholesome food but also teaches your children valuable lessons about budgeting and smart shopping.

Incorporating these apps into your routine can transform the way you approach meal preparation and family budgeting. With a little bit of planning and the right tools at your fingertips, you can create a harmonious balance between healthy eating and financial responsibility. Embrace the convenience of technology, and watch as it empowers you to nourish your family while staying within your budget. The journey to healthier eating and smarter spending can be enjoyable and fulfilling, paving the way for a happier, healthier family life.

11

Chapter 11: Conclusion and Next Steps

Embracing a Healthy Lifestyle

Embracing a healthy lifestyle is a journey that every busy parent can embark on, regardless of their hectic schedules and financial constraints. It begins with simple changes that can be seamlessly integrated into daily routines. As families juggle work, school, and extracurricular activities, it's essential to prioritize health in a way that feels manageable and sustainable. By focusing on small, achievable goals, families can create a foundation for lasting healthy habits that not only benefit individual members but also strengthen family bonds.

One of the most effective ways to embrace a healthy lifestyle is through meal planning. This practice allows families to save both time and money while ensuring they have nutritious options readily available. By dedicating just a little time each week to plan meals, parents can avoid the stress of lastminute dinner decisions and reduce the temptation to opt for unhealthy takeout. Involving the entire family in this process can make it even more enjoyable. Kids can help choose recipes, create a shopping list, and even assist in the kitchen, fostering a sense of teamwork and excitement around healthy eating.

Another key component of a healthy lifestyle is the incorporation of physical activity into daily routines. Busy professional families can find creative ways to stay active together. Whether it's a family walk after dinner, a weekend bike ride, or a fun dance-off in the living room, moving together not only promotes physical health but also strengthens family relationships. Choosing activities that everyone enjoys makes it easier to stay consistent, turning exercise into a fun family tradition rather than a chore.

Healthy eating doesn't have to break the bank. There are numerous budget-friendly options that make nutritious choices accessible to families. Embracing seasonal produce, buying in bulk, and planning meals around sales can significantly reduce grocery bills while ensuring meals are wholesome and satisfying. Additionally, cooking at home opens up a world of possibilities for creativity and experimentation in the kitchen. Families can explore new recipes together, discovering delicious and healthy meals that fit their tastes and budget.

Ultimately, embracing a healthy lifestyle is about making choices that align with family values and goals. It's about creating an environment where health is prioritized, not just in terms of food and exercise, but also in mental and emotional well-being. By supporting one another in this journey, families can cultivate a culture of health that lasts for generations. Remember, every small step counts, and together, you can create a vibrant, healthy lifestyle that is both enjoyable and sustainable.

Encouragement for Busy Medical Professionals

As busy medical professionals, finding the time to prepare healthy meals can feel like an overwhelming task amidst the chaos of daily life. Juggling work, children's school activities, and family commitments often leaves little room for meal planning. However, it's vital to remember that nourishing your family doesn't have to be a complicated or time-consuming endeavor. Simplifying your approach can help you create nutritious meals without stress, allowing you to focus on what truly matters: spending quality time with your loved ones.

Embrace the power of meal preparation as a strategy to save time and money. Set aside a few hours each week to plan and prepare your meals. Involve your kids, if any, in this process; not only will it teach them valuable skills, but it can also become a fun family activity. Choose recipes that can be made in batches, such as soups, stews, or casseroles, and store them in individual portions. This way, on those busy weekdays, you can simply reheat a wholesome meal, eliminating the temptation to resort to takeout.

Remember that healthy eating doesn't require expensive ingredients. Focus on budget-friendly staples like beans, whole grains, and seasonal vegetables, which are often both nutritious and affordable. By shopping at local farmers' markets or using store loyalty programs, you can find fresh produce at lower prices. Explore the world of frozen fruits and vegetables as well; they are picked at peak ripeness and can be just as nutritious as fresh options, providing you with versatility and ease in meal preparation.

Try to cultivate a positive mindset about food as a family. Encourage your children to explore new flavors and textures while making mealtimes a relaxed and enjoyable experience. Involve them in choosing recipes and cooking, allowing them to express their creativity. Establishing a routine around family meals can foster connections and open conversations, reinforcing the importance of healthy eating habits without the pressure of perfection.

Lastly, be kind to yourself. It's perfectly okay to have days when things don't go as planned. Celebrate your successes, no matter how small, and recognize that you are doing your best to provide for your family. Healthy eating is a journey, not a destination. By making small, manageable changes and staying committed to nurturing your family's well-being, you are paving the way for a lifetime of healthy habits. Remember, every effort counts, and you set a wonderful example for your children to follow.

Looking Ahead: Future Meal Planning

As busy parents, the daily hustle often leaves little time for meal planning, but looking ahead can significantly ease the stress of feeding your family. By setting aside a few moments each week to map out your meals, you can not only save time but also cultivate healthier eating habits for your loved ones. Consider creating a meal plan that aligns with your family's schedule, utilizing weekends or quieter evenings to brainstorm ideas that cater to everyone's tastes while remaining budget friendly.

A great starting point for future meal planning is to involve the entire family in the process. Engage your children in choosing recipes, making it a fun activity that sparks their interest in healthy eating. Encourage them to select a couple of new dishes each week, allowing everyone to contribute to the menu. This collaborative approach not only fosters a sense of ownership but also helps children develop their culinary skills and an appreciation for nutritious ingredients, making mealtime more enjoyable for all.

Another effective strategy is to embrace batch cooking and meal prep. Dedicate a few hours on weekends to cook larger portions of your favorite meals, which can then be stored for quick weekday dinners. This not only saves time but also reduces the temptation to resort to unhealthy takeout options on busy nights. By preparing versatile ingredients like grains, proteins, and vegetables in advance, you can mix and match them throughout the week to create diverse meals without the daily pressure of cooking from scratch.

Keep an eye on seasonal produce and local sales to maximize your budget while planning meals. Seasonal fruits and vegetables are typically more affordable and packed with flavor, making them a perfect addition to your weekly menu. By incorporating these ingredients into your meal planning, you not only support local agriculture but also expose your family to a variety of flavors and nutrients that can boost overall health. This approach encourages creativity in the kitchen as you adapt your recipes to whatever is fresh and available.

Finally, remember to stay flexible with your meal plans. Life with young children can be unpredictable, and it's essential to adjust your plans as needed. If a particular dish doesn't turn out as expected or your schedule changes, don't hesitate to swap meals around or repurpose leftovers. The key to successful meal planning lies in its adaptability, allowing you to keep meals fresh and exciting while still prioritizing health and budget considerations. Embrace this journey, knowing that each small step you take toward mindful meal planning contributes to a healthier, happier family.

Resources

Eating healthily starts with smart shopping choices! Use this grocery list as a guide to stock your kitchen with nutrient-dense, whole foods while avoiding processed and unhealthy ingredients.

Fruits & Vegetables (Fresh or Frozen)

Apples, oranges, bananas, berries (strawberries, blueberries, raspberries)

Avocados, mangoes, pears, grapes, pineapples

Leafy greens (spinach, kale, romaine, arugula)

Carrots, bell peppers, cucumbers, zucchini, squash

Broccoli, cauliflower, Brussels sprouts

Sweet potatoes, regular potatoes

Onions, garlic, tomatoes

Healthy Proteins

Organic eggs

Grass-fed beef, pasture-raised poultry

Wild-caught fish (salmon, tuna, cod)

Beans and lentils

Chickpeas, hummus

Organic tofu, tempeh

Plain Greek yogurt

Raw nuts (almonds, walnuts, cashews, pecans)

Nut butters (no added sugar or oils)

Healthy Fats

Extra virgin olive oil

Coconut oil

Grass-fed butter or ghee

Chia seeds, flaxseeds, hemp seeds

Whole Grains & Healthy Carbs

Quinoa, brown rice, wild rice

Steel-cut or rolled oats

Whole grain or sprouted bread

Whole grain pasta

Almond flour, coconut flour

Ezekiel bread

Dairy & Dairy Alternatives

Full-fat, organic dairy products (milk, cheese, yogurt)

Unsweetened almond, coconut, or oat milk

Pantry Staples

Organic canned beans (black beans, chickpeas, lentils)

Low-sodium vegetable, chicken, or beef broth

Organic tomato sauce, diced tomatoes

Apple cider vinegar, Balsamic vinegar

Herbs & spices (turmeric, cinnamon, oregano, basil)

Himalayan pink salt or sea salt

Raw honey or pure maple syrup (in moderation)

Dark chocolate (70% cacao or higher)

Healthy Snacks

Air-popped popcorn

Hard-boiled eggs

Trail mix (with raw nuts, seeds, and unsweetened dried fruit)

Fresh fruit with nut butter

Rice cakes with avocado or hummus

Veggies with guacamole or hummus

No-sugar-added applesauce

The 2024 Dirty Dozen List

When possible, especially if consumed frequently, buy organic for these items. Remember most farmers markets are great sources for delicious organic produce at peak ripeness - and it's a great way to support local farmers! These items are loaded with vitamins, minerals and fiber, so if you can't afford organic, don't skip them! Simply rinse the items under rushing water, then soak in warm water for a minimum of one minute. Although the peel often contains a great deal of nutrients (such as in apples), consider peeling items if you consume them frequently.

- ➤ Strawberries

- ➤ Spinach

- ➤ Kale, collard & mustard greens

- ➤ Grapes

- ➤ Peaches

- ➤ Pears

- ➤ Nectarines

- ➤ Apples

- ➤ Bell and hot peppers

- ➤ Cherries

- ➤ Blueberries

- ➤ Green beans

The 2024 Clean 15 List

Conventionally farmed versions of these items are generally safe to consume. Of course, if you have the option of buying them from a local farmer's market or raising your own - that's even better! And don't forget, even if they are organic, it's still important to rinse them well before consuming.

- ➤ Carrots
- ➤ Sweet potatoes
- ➤ Mangoes
- ➤ Mushrooms
- ➤ Watermelon
- ➤ Cabbage
- ➤ Kiwi
- ➤ Honeydew melon
- ➤ Asparagus
- ➤ Sweet peas
- ➤ Papaya
- ➤ Onions
- ➤ Pineapple
- ➤ Sweet corn
- ➤ Avocados

Tips for Healthier Shopping

Read ingredient labels – Avoid added sugars, hydrogenated oils, artificial sweeteners, and preservatives.

Shop the perimeter – The healthiest foods are usually around the edges of the grocery store.

Choose organic when possible – Especially for the "Dirty Dozen" (high pesticide produce like strawberries and spinach).

Meal prep in advance – Wash and chop veggies, cook grains, and portion out healthy snacks.

Use this guide to make healthier choices and set yourself and your family up for better nutrition and long-term wellness!

Author's Bio

Jane Moughon is a "Healthy Eating Vibrant Living" teacher, author, and group/personal coaching leader. She empowers individuals to take control of their health by teaching the impact of nutrition, vitamin and mineral deficiencies, and how they affect overall well-being. With over 25 years of studying supplements, alternative health, and nutrition, she guides parents, medical professionals, and people from all walks of life who want to break free from the cycle of processed foods, pharmaceuticals, and a system that treats symptoms rather than root causes.

Jane cares deeply about you and your family's health. Her mission is to help you prepare fast, fresh, and nutritious meals while making food preparation a fun and engaging family activity.

Find more health and nutrition insights on my Facebook page, Jane Boyd Moughon, and join my private Facebook group, Healthy Eating Vibrant Living, for exclusive tips and community support.

Stay tuned for my upcoming books in English and Spanish!

For health and nutrition training, group coaching, or personalized coaching for support and accountability, email me at

Jane@gethealthiercoach@gmail.com.

https://www.facebook.com/groups/976294634219883